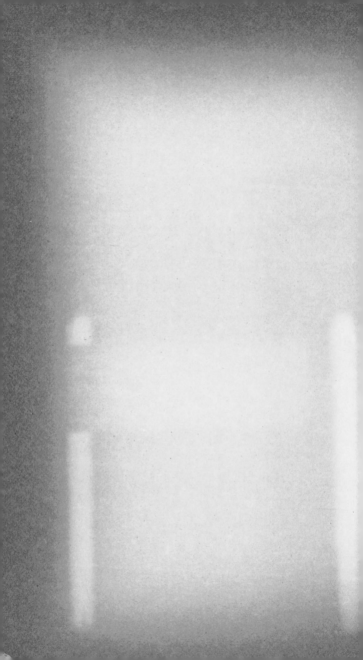

LESS
THAN A SCORE,
BUT A POINT

LESS THAN A SCORE, BUT A POINT

POEMS BY
T. J. REDDY

VINTAGE BOOKS
A Division of Random House   New York

VINTAGE BOOKS EDITION August 1974
First Edition
Copyright © 1971, 1974 by T. J. Reddy

Grateful acknowledgment is made to Moore Publishing
Company for permission to reprint "To the Bright
Bystanders" by T. J. Reddy, which appeared in their
publication *A Galaxy of Black Writing*, 1970.

Library of Congress Cataloging in Publication Data

Reddy, T   J   1945-
  Less than a score, but a point; poems.

  I. Title.
PS3568.E343L4   811'.5'4   74-7173
ISBN 0-394-71080-0

This book is dedicated to my great-grandmother, Mrs. Ella Ruffin, whose caring and guidance gave me access to an unselfish knowledge and loving sensitivity, and to Mama, the oldest living relative of my ancestral family, who made it possible, in a repressive and poverty-stricken environment, for me to have a rich and happy upbringing that money or material cannot measure. To Mama, who has been a purposeful inspiration to continue learning and loving, to be humanly true to my Black self and my creativity in the midst of adversity and when all odds have been against me.

CONTENTS

LESS
THAN A SCORE,
BUT A POINT

1. Time Out—While Caged In

3

LESS THAN A SCORE, BUT A POINT

This is another year in the end of a decade
Since we tend to think more in numbers
But not of certain terms

Ten decades ago this thing called race was
Still in the running and rising like
A swelling and smelling sore
A decade ago wounded Black and white eyes kept
    seeing
Lives end from bombs fires ropes and lies
And the blood of war over here over there
Hardly has any time to dry before hearts grow eyes
And see reddrops are all the same color

Last year was the end of a decade
I went down to the health department to give blood
And thought if someone white used it
I would ask to have it back. Black Indian giver
they call me
If they knew Black blood
Was life in their bodies would they die anyway?
I can hold no life against them except their own

Racist idolatry rests on pink skin and Black blood
This should be the end of these lifelong ills
Since we tend to think about living
Only when we run and breathe faster than usual.

WHAT COLOR IS LIFE?

I come to enlighten
In the dark
To a place that is full
Of space
What color is life?
Let me be your renaissance
I am an art
I come to paint sound
Listen—
Learn how to hear
I speak to you
Through my dark chamber

ANCIENT THOUGHTS

I

I leave written ways
The road marks signal me to
Think the things aloud.

II
The sky swirled the eye
Puffs above the stormy vision
Cloudy patterns mesh.

III
Deep frightful the dark
  Kept curled near the snoozing light
Dreams too have limits.

NOCTURNAL #1

But it wasn't too much
                    to witness
with closed eyes
                stainglass thoughts
                spiritual remnants
Cotton candy happenings
                    spun in
my sleeping head
              dream scenes with whirlwind speed
                  And me
              waking up thinking
            I could have a photo
                  graph
                of it all
              on my pillow

POET BLACKCHILD

Blackchild
          said
I
wish
I
was
     a feather
     dipped in a cloud bucket
     so it could
     design the sky with my color

ON STUPORS

Thunder showers soak hot soil
Inhaling winds suck curtains
To the window screen
Small fountains form
Where raindrops die
And swell into puddles
That rush to curbs
Like old wine and alcohol
Water from a drunk
Instruments of sensation
Play on a dirty skin

Thoughts are flushed
But not the wounded memories—

The key to more room is locked in the closet
It is a help that hurts
A reach too short
It is cries of hunger
Quieted with a poison spoon
It is like eyes
That cannot retain a vision
It is distance
Too far gone to go back

What do you say
Silent speaker?

TO THE BRIGHT BYSTANDERS

Shelter from the shade
A trip to the penny arcade
Where pinballs and cue sticks
Trade licks with each other
   For a prize

Prize one you think
For giving you the game
Prize none for playing

You win you lose
A trip to sunshine maybe
Sometime, you may get brighter

OUT OF AFRICA'S EDEN

I am history
My life goes back to Africa
For its beginnings

Snatched out of my mother's knifeslit womb
Into the grasp of a smothering white fist
I am squeezed, thrown to the ground
Stomped into a lifeless pulp or
Stuck with the stench of death in a slave ship
After being baited netted
Dragged through a sea of
My sisters' and my brothers' blood
Out of it I emerge: Love

I am dawn, a new day, the sun
I am Xhosa and Ibo and Zulu
I am Hottentot and Bushman

I am dusk
Son of night
Preserved in my shadows
Rediscovering visions lost
Reclaiming my sights

I am survival, daytime, nighttime

I am Hottentot poem,
   "Their bones are far
   Their souls wander
   Are they far away, or are they close?
   Do they want sacrifice, or do they want
      blood . . . ?"

I am Bushman poem, "Prayer to the Moon,"
   "Did you not promise us once
      that we should return and be happy after death?"

I am history
My death, the basis of oppressors' wealth
Having died fetus and centenarian I live as a poem
Preserving my livelihood, my ancestry, my heritage,
My freedom, my spirituality
Black and strong.

POEMS OF HISTORY

Black spokesmen/women long ago
Back when we lived
Buried alive in the seams
of American history books
Books Black people learned to read
In the fields, in the pines,

In the dark
Then

When not so tied down or
Hung up in ignorance
And having learned how to know
To find our way
To see how to be free
We turned to writing poetry
A privilege once reserved for whites only

Goddamn nigras writin 'bout
what we do,
Black nerve!
We nevah shoulda
   Give 'em learnin

But we found our way
Out of shackling, hanging seams
And versed our cry for freedom
In poems of Black experience,
Poems of history,
Black people poems
From the first lines of Lucy Terry
To George Moses Horton, Frances E. W. Harper,
James Weldon Johnson, Paul Lawrence Dunbar,
Claude McKay, Jean Toomer, Countee Cullen
Right on down to the blues poems
Of Langston Hughes.
Black people poems
Like freedom songs

Gospel truth poems
To live with spiritually.

"Godamn nigras writin 'bout
what we do—Look see!
Black nerve!

Now they talk about
Freedom from slavery.

We nevah shoulda
Let 'em live
Or give 'em
Learnin.''

WHAT NEXT
To Gustavus Vassa*

———————————————————————

thick sticky spit
surrounds
still Black mouths
seasalt stains
Black skins
already covered with mud

———————————————————————

* Gustavus Vassa was the name given by one of his
owners to Olaudah Equiano, an Ibo slave whose *Equiano's
Travels: The Interesting Narrative of the Life of Olaudah
Equiano or Gustavus Vassa the African*, published in 1789,
was one of the first books written by an African in English.

silent halfdead eyes
look on in disbelief

shoulder to shoulder
suffering Black eyes
look deep past
each other's waste
wondering what next
will call the cough
of a Black life up,
or sputter out
the safest bloodsong
the swiftest bloodsong
the swiftest and sweetest
way to die

not as a slave . . . drown overboard
not as a slave . . . starve
not as a slave . . . swallow the tongue
not as a slave . . . kill the children
not as a slave . . . the beauty of horror
down
down
down
in the belly of a wooden beast's
indigestion
choking on the morbid air
breathing over and over again
each other's waste
wondering to death
what next

TO BROTHER VAN LIEROP

Realizing that just because it is centuries later
does not make the pain of oppression end
You, with camera, with pen, with voice bring together
what it is about today that is worth noticing
about the past and how it oppresses us

I didn't get to tell you what I thought
of your time here. Knowing how much the truth
of our life and death is hidden under
contradictions, discrepancies, hypocrisies,
distortions, lies, call them what you will—
knowing how much the truth is denied us
about our past, our history, ancestry, heritage
it did me good to have a new dimension added to
my understanding of the future when you came into it

It is first our ignorance of what oppresses us
that keeps our minds and bodies enslaved
Freedom is a state of mind to be realized
in terms of what we know of attempts to destroy us

A Mozambican sun rising on your brow, you awaken
in our eyes the hills of a Motherland that
gives her breast as mountains and as shelter
for Black babies to live and grow knowing freedom,
a Motherland that gives her warmth, the sun,
her tears, the rain, her life, the land
that gives us the future as freedom

To Brother Van Lierop, recording history
in the faces of the people, fighting, struggling,
reflecting, smiling, caring, knowing—
Now is no time to wait for liberation.

MAMA THE REVOLUTIONARY

Saw the blackest woman
   Pink kerchief
Bent a knot into a bow
Across her brow
She looked like
   Ah you know
Instead of pancakes
She handles a gun

TO A BLACK AESTHETIC

You have let me
feel your way
Let me be caressed
immersed, loved by you
You are life's experience
Ebony encounter
moonbright in darkness
a dream come true

I came to know beauty
was me, my Blackness
lovely, loving how you came

I have felt
your movement under me
revealed deeply, tenderly.

TO THE AUDIENCE IN THE ARENA

To the scratched walls, the digging catpaws, splinter
   of life falling
On a sod floor, a Black baby standing barefoot in the
   door of a shack
Holding a pot of halfcooked weekold rice

I used to look for answers in a set of 40 year old
   encyclopedias and
Laughed coldly at a classmate who wore pajamas
   under his pants
(we were kinda in jail he told me) I can't beat my
   conga drums no more
Cops say too much noise disturbs the peace and
   where has the dust
That made me guard my eyes settled? Ever touch old
   flesh? I saw a starving baby
Die on TV. Another friend of mine wanted to make
   love with his own.

You know, he said, but she did. The sheets were dingy and grey with

Body dirt and age. But she slid under him anyway.

Kids are getting smarter. Asked one if he knew better and he asked me

The same question. The news belongs to 6 o'clock and screen soldiers,

The same yesterday eyes, a book on great decisions at the end of the year.

You a hippie, you in school? a dropper on my scene asked. No, I said,

I'm trying to teach you something. Too much, too much man, he said, too much.

Fear, are you my real friend? I hear the crime of injustice is not so bad. Expectations,

You don't sedate me like you once did. You've accumulated like my questions.

It's like a child asking what is life and being given a sentence

Until he finds out the hard way. Then maybe he will know

What sociological implications there are in a comic strip, a cartoon

And learn the definition of epistemology. Goodbye acknowledgments,

Wall posters, last year's birthdays, purple hearts, and curricula.

I can't stop thinking about the dead roaches on the toilet seat

And the retarded child who was asked what he would do if he couldn't

Get his pants on over his shoes and get a bigger
   pair of pants
Was not the right answer. Get out. I am sick of
   smelling
Your breath and sweat, hearing your growling
   stomach, tired of
Your interest, concentration camps, ignorance, vote-
   getting speeches
Your castrations. I'm not trying to think any more.
Dear Rob, I'm stealing to create and stay alive.
They don't like poetry and curse words, but look in
   the consumer guide
To show them how. Spring, why do you hurt so bad
   and where are you?

DIRT END

Its difficult to tell
by looking at the stains
If someone Black or white
Used the wash basin
The s
     i
       n
         k
Gets all our dirt
soon enough

THE SADNESS THAT SEEPS THROUGH
BRICK AND SAND

Getting stripes for being good old soldiers
a good used deal a magic mixer a cold drink
something to soothe results
of pulling and scraping
the lacerations that are made by points sliding
through to the bone
the sadness that seeps and drips from Black bodies
burned into shambles
a sliding board that doesn't want to end
a swing in a kinetic way
happiness as evidence of a deadlive love
the sadness that seeps through
thicket and trash
knowing you weren't born yesterday
or what a birthday is without you
being a sucker thinking sweet things stink
the sadness that bricks up and blocks with swift
    blows

Like pugilists we take our stand
combatantly trying to spare our heads or hearts
and the hard core that is so soft
isn't even there

SENILE BRANDS
or, FOR 70-YEAR-OLD COWBOYS

Life's hum strum along
Becomes a strain on
Old cowboy lungs
Like untuned guitar strings,
Rusty now

Yodels muffled, gargled,
Shaky like
The sound of some
Faraway stampede
Fading in the sunset

Tired cowboys talk of guitar girlfriends
Dry gulch saloons
Yesteryear bronco rodeo shows

Voices that once galloped now trot
Weary of memories of having roamed the range
Over longgone prairies and trails

They ride their rockingchair stallions,
Rope dreams with threadbare blankets
Steak dinners now soups
and mashed beans,
Deadeye whiskey
now milk of magnesia

They drink from a stream of
                    deep
                    thought
Cowboy vikings wake without oars
With corrals built around
Their prairie rest homes
Thinking they were responsible
For rock and roll and the miniskirt
Trying to forget the effort
With tobacco pouch strings
Slipping through tired gums

Trigger fingers only good now
For buttoning warm underwear.

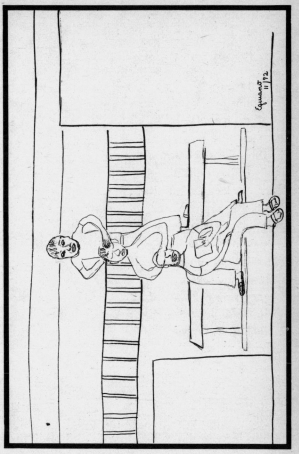

2. Braiding Hair, Reading Scene

WHITE TEMPLES

Lights
    Not many
Face shining
    Madeup smile
White spats
    On calloused Black feet
Shuffle across the stage
At another last curtain

Banjo John he was called
Doing nothing in his life
But dancing to songs
In segregated theatres
Always trying to show
How grateful he was
How important he was
To be allowed in
Even as a nigger

He figured to make
his living
Making his non-Black audience
Happy
Knowing that for half a century
He had hidden the abuses
in his eyes

Offstage
    Hat in hand
The song and dance
    Routine over
His brother's children said
It was easy to call him uncle.

STITCHES

The chill that catches my skin
and sends the vibration my mind feels
The patch of sun from a crack
In the curtain just faded—sometimes
It's cold inside the house I carry with me
I don't worry about growing old
    Suddenly my thoughts
will hold out to hand me
what I can't understand
I've seen the rain on old men's eyes
It can be difficult to go out
When we are almost already there
So death doesn't frighten me
Life does
I've stopped to look at my hands
and can't count the lines I've added
to them
I know the patches in my past
Can come loose within me

INTO MY HANDS I POCKET TEARS

On the 4th floor
Of a ghetto building
Nineyearold Black youth od's

Glass syringe splinters
Tinkles
Tumbles down four flights
Of roach and rat shitted
Worn down pissed on stairs

Black child stumbles
Slumps to the railing
Where his lifeless body lands

He drops his wideopen
White no pupiled
Dead terrified eyes
Into my hands

AFALSIONADO

They couldn't tell from looking
at the silhouette on the shade
if he was Black or white
Couldn't tell if the kinks in his hair

were straight or curly,
Couldn't tell the color of his skin
or if there was any particular
characteristic that could distinguish
him from them. And they were afraid
to shoot into the window for fear of
killing themselves.

DR. DEATH THE COMMUNITY PHYSICIAN

The white death dust dopes our eyes
Blinding us to the future of our lives
White death dust like a metallic fog
In our nostrils, lungs and veins
Crystallizes, clogs

Dr. Death the murdering magician
Displays disaster
He needles Black neighborhoods while
Dressed in surgical robes
He is the executioner as community physician
Selling little bags called "trays"
And what he calls with a smile
"Nigger goody headache powders"

Dr. Death sells the neighborhood
On making a profit

Some of us end up spent
The goody turning our brains to cement

I've seen on the westside streets here
Corners filled with glassy-yellow
Wateryeyed brothers sniffing Dr. Death's dope
Into their noses
And on the southside
You can find Black youth
In the midst of heavy traffic
Getting run down run over
By pushers dealing bags of scag
More like bags of scabs
Because the sores this sickness
Leaves on us just don't want
To heal too fast

The drug traffic here takes its toll
While driving through this city's westside one night
I almost ran over a brother
His body huddled over in the middle
Of the street
Needle full of blood
Hanging from his arm
His mouth slobbering
His eyes fixed on the car's headlights
I flashed up from dim
In his standstill fascination with the glare
I almost ran over him

Dr. Death the political magician
Needles Black neighborhoods

Selling death for a profit
At the expense of Black people's lives

THE NATIVE

Longhaired no bra breast and naked
Dancers of dreams
Hear me, silent noise makers
High minded explorers of the future
Get into the veins of your mind
About my freedom
And how drugs exclude me
Keep in touch with yourself
There are jungles full of joneses
I too feel native and restless
Because of habits

LOVE ON MOVEMENT

With the shortcomings
I came willfully
making my way to you

All is taken with
the step

you and I both know
Never one foot
at a time
But with a pace
that packs movement
in every turn

You
          are
     a   motion
and I realize
with my weary trailing eyes
How I still sense the dynamics of
your freedom as mine

SWEAT DADDY'S DAYS

When that 'mancipation thing passed
it failed
for the way Sweat Daddy felt
he knew
ain't no way constipashun
could set you free

Sweat Daddy say he'd wait
for more than just a word
but you know
that saltstained black skin of his

faded in the seasons of far gone times
times he was forgotten in
but could not be overlooked in
then Sweat Daddy's
skin
fell
off
but his body still stood
for more
still raw
still restless
in rotting anticipation
waiting for more promises
of white freedom
then
Sweat Daddy's
flesh
fell
off

Black bones weathered battered
and naturally
still in bare facts
knowing
of more 'mancipationlikethings
much much better than
what the one
passed
was suppose to do
then
Sweat Daddy's

statement
died
the day he made it
y'all
who call nothing ALL

what good is freedom
Sweat Daddy say
if
you
got
to
be
dead
to
be
'mancipated

DISCOVERY IN THE BRUSH

American abstract artist
Cannot figure why his brush paints unexpectedly
a three-linked chain casting slanting shadows
Images silhouetting the canvas with faces
Of Modiglianni, Picasso, and Miro.
He tries calling transatlantic
To the interior of Africa
For an interpretation.

I've warped the wayside with my stride and glide

gone to ditches hitched in darkness
fallen in afraid of white fangs and fire
I've warped the wayside
with my reach and leap
fallen out afraid of blackteeth and lye
this image on the back of my mind
a piercing thought
bent and curved like a crescentcradle
I've warped the ditches hitched in blackness
and come with myself to see

CLUTCH POEM

Like a siamese cat caught
Between two worlds
Pulled east and west
She lurks with paws outstretched
Shown concern she scratches, claws
She climbs walls
Slides down curtains
And rips the velvet
Air to shreds
She hisses howls and meows
Leaps from tables to chairs
She sleeps in corners

Wanting hurt to feed on
Hate she deems love
The house struggles
To redeem her
She wants to heal wounds
With salt and more scratches
She has learned how
To carry a leash
To those she wants
To walk away with her
She runs after mirages
And false oases on a desert
Her laughter is a frightened shadow
Life tries to make her real
She flees from this need
I hardly slept last night
The hissing heavy on my ears
I heard her hate and fear again
Lacerate the air.

RAW FEELING

The tune of early blues
Kept my ear
to the sound

When I was a little boy
The music did me good

When I was a little older
The sound skipped my mind
The BLUES is back
To stay up front
I like it
Like a man blue
Black night of sound
I remember your song
And put my foot
Lightly to the floor
And got rhythm
From my moves
Pleasure from my grooves
I've grown up
Feelin raw without you.

RUNNING UPON A WALL

When I was attending a socalled
Negro university as a colored track student
Going around in circles and getting
Nowhere at different places
All the time
I ended up in a Black slum
Outside the screen gate wall
Where colored classroom curriculum
Closed its sight to the eyesore
Society's educational institutions
Helped produce

While I attended this institution
I learned that I was to learn
Good colored college sense
And the social graces of
White America designed for Black people
To slowly exterminate themselves with—
I learned I was to keep my mind so preoccupied
With nonsense there was no time
For free thinking

After running miles into the community
I wiped thick saliva from the corners
Of my mouth
Wiped my confused
Sweating forehead and rubbed
My smarting eyes as I looked deeply
Into the gaze of an old Blackman
Who sat alone in a debris strewn field
Holding a bottle of wine with both hands

I saw rag and sore covered bodies
Saw the weary faces of Black people
Whose eyes told me to run
Run fool run
Run fool run
Run fast as you can for help to that place
Written across the front of that sweatsuit
You are wearing
Run their eyes told me
Run to that college of higher learning
And get some help
For the Black people in this community

I was as isolated as the slum community
When I found the privileged Black students
Didn't want to do anything
Outside of the classroom
Unless they got extra credit for it

The importance of teaching at college
Dawned on me in those streets
I learned at once how college classrooms were
    largely responsible
For the institutional wounds
Ignorance poverty and disease
Being educated help inflict

DISTANCE GOING NOWHERE

Stopped the car
On one hell of a hot day
Three sunburned white boys
With thumbs on fire
Stood there wondering
Because the front seat
    A Black seat

"Look," I said,
"Got no time for you
Wanna ride, get in
If you don't
Turn loose my handle."

One little white blister
Said, "Shit, I'd rather walk first."
Maybe his mama told him
"Don't ride with strangers."
And the other two were confused
When their kin said
"Black folk don't count."

I told the one
who had rather walk,
"Boy, you better learn how to walk,
You'd better learn before your behind drags off,
You'd better learn rides for free
Don't come Black or white but fast,
You'd better learn to ride with me
Or get out from under my wheels
So
I won't have to run over you."

JUDGE POEM

Judge said I am something of a romantic
And, yes, I confess I am
I love life, I love love
And I am romantic minded
Knowing that in the midst
Of all the hatred and death
My love of life is all I have left

Judge said I am something of a romantic
That my poetry is used
To mold people's minds to malicious ends
But judge never heard my poems
Read in the courtroom
He cannot afford to judge poems
His judgment trapped in his fears and prejudices

And this Mississippi-bred white boy
Who had his political hopes shattered
Is he trying to make a name for himself
As an advocate of righteousness
By being so willfully wrong,
Hiding his hatred of Black people
Behind a facade of judicial procedures

Judge said I am something of a romantic,
That he could see me leaving for Algeria
So he set bail at fifty thousand dollars
And after four appeal hearings for a bond reduction
State Supreme Court sends us back
To the judge who originally condemned us

Judge said he thinks I am intelligent, creative
Said I *had* a future
But since those voodoo dolls
Keep looming in his mind
And his fears keep mounting
Judge Snepp snips snaps at my heart
Labels me tactician, conspirator, overeducated
    revolutionary

Beyond rehabilitation
Gives me a 20-year sentence
And allows those who confess to the crime
We are accused of
To escape prosecution

Judge deals with life
In terms of lovelessness
My only crime is my love of freedom
The color of my skin
But in America's courtrooms
I am left at the mercy of laws
Designed to try me into submission

But I cannot live your lies, judge
I can't smile while you heap racist laws on me
And have you expect me to be grateful for them

Judge said I am something of a romantic
And, yes, I confess I am
I love life, I love love
And I am romantic minded
Knowing that in the midst
Of all the hatred and death
My love of life is all I have left.

I'LL NEVER LOVE A JAIL

I'm a fool for love, maybe
But fantasize or
Romanticize this cage?
I'll never love a jail

NOTES TO MISS ann
Response to an Editorial

I hold on to my claim
Long as I can
That America
Is known for burning
Breaths away
Has more concern
For horses
Kisses for kittens
Cares more
About dog shit
Than human life

DAMN, NO THANK YOU MAN

Under the circumstances it may not mean
Much to you, my humanity, pride,
Self respect, my honesty—but give it up
For freedom from this can?
Damn, no thank you man!

I understand I cannot go
To your exclusive country clubs
Or enjoy conversation about me as dollar sign
I cannot enjoy your talk of plans and schemes
Hidden persuaders for more profit
I can't enjoy leisure, luncheons, merchandising
    shows
I can't enjoy being changed for dollars
Out of my innocence
I won't be marketed, bid for
Auctioned to be free, I can't just
Close my eyes to what is destroying life and me
Or forget that a system employing murderers
To save life by killing it
Is nothing but a deathly compromise

And I realize that as long
As my mouth and hand spell freedom,
Those who want to still my movement
Will try to cut out my tongue
Cut off my fingers
Use concrete and steel

To hammer me into submission and confinement
Damn, no thank you man!

I understand that I cannot afford
To play this deadly game
Accept the rule that justice is a tool
To enslave and abuse me
I cannot afford to think
Justice will free me without giving
Up my life for more death, more abuse
More slavery

Damn, no thank you man!
I understand I cannot depend
On those who enslave me to free me
Without promising to give up
My eyes in return
How then could I be real
Knowing I accepted slavery as freedom,
Injustice as justice, and hypocrisy as equality
Knowing I kissed ass,
Had my nose like whipped dog
Dragged through shit, was spat on
Sat up for a bone, only to be
Beaten across the head with it

To you, my innocence, my honesty,
My self respect, my pride, my humanity
May not mean much
But give it up for more slavery——
Damn, no thank you man!

ISLAND CELL BLOCK

Cell block like an island
With more life than it can handle
Not enough food for too much hunger
Not enough space for too much movement
Breath gets heavier, shorter
Sensory overload develops

When hands or feet can't push
or burrow through concrete
When eyes so seldom see love or feel warmth
When heads are hung up in steel and hopelessness
The adrenalin starts flowing
Early morning headaches
come crushing down on bodies, heavily
Voices on the verge of explosion
Arguments erupt over card games:
"I got more than you'll ever have."
"That's right, you do, you got more time to serve."
A fight almost occurs.
If someone asks someone else to turn a radio down,
Somebody else turns it up louder
Others, to let off steam,
Masturbate under sheets
in the shower
on steel benches
under tables.
Cell block an island of the unlucky
Sixteen bodies crammed into space for seven

in what is called the Bull Pen
No word of relief for days
from attorney, wife, friends
And in this dull light
oppressive shadows are cast
on these Black bodies
Already broken by time,
Bodies of shattered beliefs
Looking through thick windowpanes
Bodies of eyes
Looking past concrete
to more bars
Black bodies draped, arms hanging
through steel barricades
Groping for some hope, some word

Sometimes the air gets hard here,
Hard as steel porcelain shit stalls,
Hard with anger, bitterness and rage,
Hard as the concrete hearts
Outside this cage

TO HIDE CRIES IN THE RAIN

After a breakfast of cold grits
Eggs with shell in them
Cold coffee
Cold rolls that reek of garbage cans
Inmates talk of world's tallest buildings
Conversation turns into shouting match over
Who builds the most shit

It rained yesterday, first time that
I've noticed water touch the outside
of this cell block's dirtstreaked window
Day to shower
Maybe some of the foul air
will disappear.
Inmate sings when jailer opens door,
"Wanna
go
outside
in
the
rain"

3. Nothing To Do

WHO IS THE EXECUTIONER

I take a see
That becomes turbulent
With nausea inside you

I float into your blood vessels
Into your stream of thoughtlessness
And at the feel of me your breathing
Almost stops

Who is the executioner
I scream
Inside your vertebrae
But you will not say

I move up your spine
And the love I once felt there
Hardly causes you to stir

Who is the executioner my friend
Is it you? Is it you?

Do me a favor
If there is as you say
Nothing you can do
On your next blood test
Let me out.

SOME OF WHAT I MUST ADJUST TO

This green T-shirt
too short, paint splattered blue pants
patches of mold
on the bottoms of these white plastic shoes
Shirts gray with grime and grease
One shower stall for 16 of us
Puddles of dirty water
always on the floor

Shuffled back and forth
from bunk joint to bull pen,
Having to shit with inmates
Brushing teeth, spitting, washing underwear
in nearby sink or splattering piss over you

Bible stuck between the bars
Flies and roaches in the cell
Lights out, dark 11 p.m.,
6 a.m. up again
Food pushed through holes
in metal trays, grits everyday
Eggs with shells in them
Bread with green on it
Liver mush, lots of beans
Crackers with almost every meal

Inmates standing near the windows
Their arms linger aimlessly,

Looking out on the summer
at skirts, legs, thighs of women
Oooo's and aaaah's and look at this one,
that one, bobbing up and down like dick ducks,
    quacking
Fuck this, fuck that all day long

Homosexuals, lifers often desperate,
Fierce agonies, horrors whispered, dripping
from their lips and penises

Radios on three different stations,
tv commercials, comedy shows, soap box operas

Aging men with sperm tears in their eyes
Childish temper tantrums
Senseless arguments
Anger mounting, tin trays raised
against each other

Inmates talking about getting cut loose
their prayers and hopes three times a day
Thinking about what must I do next
Some of what I must adjust to.

PRISON LOVE POEM
FOR MY FLOWER WOMAN

Rhythm carries me into my poem
I'm not alone
Love is in my limbs
Strong and longing
Strong for my woman's warmth
Longing for her flower
Filled with dew in the morning

EYES ON AN OVAL FRAME

A woman's
Too swinging
Swaying
Curvacious hips
Come past
This castrating
Window
My groin hungers
For involvement

NARCISSUS POEM

Inmate sneezes
Then wipes his nose
Under his breath
He whispers
When no one responds
To his involuntary seizure
"Bless me."

SPIRIT BREAKING TRYING TIME

Like days of old days into years ago
We had every shackled hope broken
by rejections, denials
Just to keep us quietly
hoping, praying, wishing, longing for a yes
But it seems all we got and get is no
Like days of old days fading into years
the hate and senseless hurt against us
To keep us quiet, corralled, waiting
for what turns out to be slaughter
hasn't changed that much
Break the nigger's spirit,
keep him quiet and still
Break the nigger's spirit,
and break his will to live

Break the nigger's spirit,
keep him caged and hated
Make him give in to despair and take his suffering
Break the nigger's tongue
blind his eyes from the sun
Break his neck—
that will do it
Like days of old days into years today
Break the nigger's spirit
oppressors say.

BURGAW TRIAL POEM*

In jail
There is no joy for me this a.m.
Whiteville has struck down
A few more Black ones
In Burgaw, N. C.

Last night when I heard of
The conviction, the construction

---

* On October 18, 1972, Reginald Epps, Jerry Jacobs, Connie
Tyndall, Benjamin F. Chavis, Marvin Patrick, Wayne Moore,
James McCoy, Ann Shephard and Joe Wright were sen-
tenced in Wilmington, N. C., on charges of conspiracy and
burning a grocery with an incendiary device during a
racial incident in Burgaw, N. C.

I visualized a boa in the courtroom
A smiling boa justice let loose
To force Black backs up against
The courtroom walls, the jury's box
And the judge's stand.

White boa slowly, very slowly
Eases on its underside, wrapping
Around Black wrists and necks
Its mouth hissing
Break, restrict
Suffocate all Black people—constrict.

Was there someone, Blackchild,
Who cried for freedom from justice's wrongdoing
Before the verdict
Was handed down?

Judge will not understand your tears, Blackchild
He probably smiled at your plea for freedom
You probably saw the blood dripping
From his draculean eyeteeth.

Did you hear him hiss the words,
"Little nigger girl, to show my thanks
I'll, like boa, make a break for you."

Today he will sentence your brothers.

POEM FOR C. W.

I cannot stay on your windowsill
And wait for you to wake

At midnight I slip out
Thru the pores in this cage's concrete
As nightlife's mist
I assume the shape of a bird
And make my way to your window
To hear you say in your sleep
"Be brave"

"With admiration and hope"
You sign the darkness
With your breast

I must get back to the reality
Of this cage before sunrise
I have looked on a minute
And a day passed

I want to leave a slab of concrete
Under your head
A steel bar in one of your hands
A feather in the other
I am aware of the killing air
I know I am not game

But prey for your dust, your decay
Your rust

The new day finds me out of
Your grasp
Your touch

MUMBO JUMBO

To Joe Dell,
victim of a mysterious death
in Raleigh's Central Prison
June 11, 1972.

On these 16 steel beds lie body heaps
Covered in dingy, too short sheets
Like corpses in a prison morgue

I think of Joe Dell
Known to defy oppression
With a passion
Known for refusing to suffer
Without reaction

And as a result in this state's
Main slave dungeon, Joe Dell
Was known to have his head beaten
Eyes maced, body hosed

Like Hard Rock and George Jackson,
Inmates say, Joe Dell was a strong minded brother
He was a Panther—agile, quick
He had a rap the brothers could relate to
Then in seeming good health
Joe Dell met with a mysterious death

Inmates say his "heart attack"
Drug-induced by jailers
And before his family could come to claim his
    remains
All the parts of his body
Needed to see how he really died
—heart, liver, lungs—
Had been misplaced, could not be found

Mumbo Jumbo, another Black life mysteriously
    crumbles
Out of these 16 steel beds inside this cell
Out of these 16 sometimes corpses
One heart, half alive, still swells.
I am zombie, Joe Dell, rising
From the dead in this hell.

BE BUFFOON LAUGH AT MYSELF: NO!

We sit watching *Soul!*
Feeling in the dark

for a change
Some needed inspiration
in the poems of Luciano
Music by Mwandishi
Relieved for a while of
Depression disgust despair
Feeling smiles inside me brighten
and come alive

Then
Just like what we get on the slop trays
instead of bread
In comes a cracker
Saying
"When I come in y'all bettah smile
so I can see you in the dark."

I tell him to split
I don't play with fools
Who try to tell nigger jokes
on the sly

Why must I be expected to laugh
about being called a nigger?
Like a buffoon
Make fun of myself?
Ain't nothing funny 'bout a cracker
Calling me nigger.

TIME ELUSIVE FLIES

One can make no plans here
Except to be assured
That maggots overnight
Will turn into flies

HOOKED ON LIFE

Like fish
Out of breath
In air
I keep my nose
Just above
Water here

TO TAKE SOME SMILES TO SLEEP

Friday morning makes its way
Into another weekenday
Guess I'll pack me a lunch
Spend some time with my woman
In the country
Guess I'll take a summer swim

See a few friends
Later listen to some music, jazz, some blues
While on a moonlight cruise back to where I am

Who knows better than I
That cages are realistic
I know there is no future
In a freedom to fantasize

But there's nothing wrong with visualizing
Scenes that are inside me restored and kept
Just for a change
So I can take some smiles to sleep

A CREDIT TO BLACK PEOPLE

They talk of piling
Another unhip term for fucking
They talk of conning this sucker
Robbing this lemon
About being a credit
To the race
By jiving the white man
Ripping off a coupla hundred g's
Then maybe
I hear them say
They will be able to help the cause

What cause?
Nothing about freedom mentioned
Just any cause
that gives them an excuse
To fuck over anyone and anything
They can

They talk of piling
Jiving and copping
Of laying and waiting
Breaking and entering someone's
nest or flesh.
And all the time I'm listening
I'm trying to figure
Just who do they think they are kidding?
Who do they think
They are joking and jiving?
Talking about fucking this
Conning that
Talking about being a credit to Black people
By enslaving them.

BLACK CHILDREN VISIT MODERN JAIL

From this cage
I see Black children pass in the halls
I see their eyes absorbed
In steel paneled concrete corridors

I hear them told by jailers
How modern this facility is
I see them shown guards and control towers
That regulate doors
I see them shown cameras that scan,
Microphones that hear the sounds
That cry out inside this can

Let me tell you, Blackchildren,
These robotized followers of rules
Won't let you see why we are here
They won't let you see children your age
Caged here with me
They won't let you hear the screams
Or see the bloodstained floors
They won't let you understand
Why 85% of those caged here
Are Black bodies like mine, like yours

Black children visit modern jail
Hurriedly they move along in a line
Huddled close side by side
Can they see they too are caged
Can they see themselves captives
Of classrooms learning ignorance
Can they see themselves captured
By American lies?

Black children I can see
How "criminal" you are forced to be

For stepping out of line to be free
From the lies
Like me

FLOWER CHILDREN POEM
To Happy and Joey

Every bed here now
Has a body chained to it
Full to capacity this cage
And before the sun rises
Dissension begins to steam
in the stifling air
Leaving these
dirt dust blood stained walls
Sweating with seething tongues
Spewing syllables of hate

I am content to let
The pingpong of disgust
Transpire without me
My peace will be the sunrise
My eyes will be absorbed
In the quiet beauty
of a flower
That two children sent
Here for me

INSECTS SINCE I'VE BEEN HERE . . . MULTIPLIED

The roaches and flies
Since I've been in this dungeon
Caged inside this cell
Multiplied
Can't understand how some inmates
Get so used to it they don't flinch
When insects crawl on them

I remember
Years ago, my involvement
With a health condition survey
In one of the city's Black communities
Undergoing "redevelopment"—
which means of course
Black people moved, relocated
From cityplanned slums and ghettos
Into another concentration camp
Closer to the central city,
near the bus line
police department
downtown stores
And where Black folks lived
now there are big office buildings
Hotels, stores, a white church
and whiteowned businesses

I remember an old Black woman
One of the last "relocatees"
It was winter time
and cold, damn cold
no heat except
the wood she tore off
the side of the shack
she called home
and burned in fivegallon
metal cans to keep
the freeze off
her Black back
No place for her to be located
No food except
Welfare meal, flour, water
"No one goes to the surplus food place
for me like they use to," she says

Large tumor on the old woman's neck
"Been there for years.
Doesn't hurt," she says,
and adds: "I tried
to get the swelling down
with a hot needle
and all it did
was get bigger."

On the floor behind the door,
on the shelves in the kitchen
like inside this dungeon
lockup cage cellblock

roaches, flies
Multiplied

I remember a compost
left for weeks
in a covered garbage can
when opened sent a zillion z's
the sound of a sawblade buzzing
down the nape of my neck
down the line of my spine

I've seen bluebottle flies
near pig stys
and now I know
why this place is called a pen.
The insects I've seen
Inside this dungeon lockup cage cellblock
Multiplied
Are not as large as the dragon types
that infest life outside
The struggle to survive insects
continues,
old Black woman,
if we live inside cages or out.

THE MISSING SPOON

Spoon missing
11 of us in cell block
10 spoons counted. Trustee tallying
trays, cups and spoons. Mistakes
known to have happened,
spoons sticking together, jailers miscounting

Waiting for the shakedown again
Strip, search, bunk hunt
looking thru your books, letters
Waiting for the shakedown
"Where did you get this penny?"
"How this Afro-comb get in here?"
"No styrofoam cups allowed!"
Sheriff, jailer says, will come
if we don't find the spoon

Jailer peeks his head thru trap door hole
And in less than it seems a second yells
"Spoon was found in another cell."
The feed hole slammed
Blam—him gone.

DAY AFTER THANKSGIVING TO NO AVAIL

Fourth appeal for bond reduction turned down today

How do you put into a poem
Written from a jail, No change
How do you write that
All efforts made toward freedom
Have been made to no avail

Freedom before it reaches me, cut short
How many more pages of Future Shock
Can I read
Before the clock stops
And my hands whirl off

I've seen inside this cage
How inmates are forced into rage
I've seen how we are provoked
Into retaliating against abuse and slavery
And how oppressors use our efforts toward freedom
As a justification for our destruction

Fourth appeal for a bond reduction made
How do you put into a poem
Written from a jail, No change
How do you write that
All efforts made toward freedom
Have been made to no avail

OUTDOOR CAGE WOMAN

I see artificiality in a tissue paper smile
A smile so superficial
You can see right thru it

The few tears intending to be sadness
Seem as if they were put on
Like false eyelashes

I want to get back to the cage
To read more than I see in stares
Gargoyle-like glances
Shrouded in fleshy eyes flitting
With a fear of age
Flesh that crumbles bit by bit
When something real touches it

The "well we can do nothing for you" face
Questions me
Wanting to know how I feel about
"The human bond"
Not wanting to confront
The bind I am in

The wrinkled lips that say
"Ooooohhh it's so good
To see you smile"
I am not happy
I am smiling

At what is talking to me
I almost want to growl
I smile

I want to get back to the cell block
It has less steel and concrete
Than your facade

The concern standing before me
Is as artificial as flowers
reeking of dust
And decay
When I need real ones to touch

A LOVE CALL REACHES MY EAR

A love call reaches the ear
of a loving woman
Waiting
For love to come home
Instead of calling in

I need to belong to someone
Woman
Woman who needs my loving smile
I need a while to recollect
Moments
Without feeling bitterness
overpowering my love

Summer foliage, orange blossom smells
Not here
Night's green glistening
Not here

When it comes to fragrance
All I get
Is breathing the odor
Of some unclean body's
Breath and sweat

A love call has reached me
From a woman
Reaching out
Touching me with love
From many miles away
Her voice gently
caresses my ear

A love call reaches my ear
From a loving woman
Waiting
For love to come home
Instead of calling in

TWO SCENES—SUMMER
THANKSGIVING POEM

I've not smelled the sweetness of honeysuckle
Nor felt love juice as it flows
On my fingers
I've not seen the skinsmooth covering
Or the blossom of a mimosa tree
I've not felt fresh air
Without high walls holding it
I've not seen river brook stream
Or rainbow prism from a waterfall
I've not seen fish swim in a silver lake
I've not felt the rain bathe my face
I've not seen a field of clover
Nor walked along a treelined road

I've seen desolation in the streets
From this cage
I've seen cars pass
With grimacing faces in them
I've seen asphalt and buildings
With windows showing curtains
And more grimaces

I've seen days come, nights fall
Felt the icy stillness inside
These clamorous stupefying walls
I've heard voices inhale sigh shift
Tumble crash and explode screaming

I've not seen the sun but once in a month
Nor felt its brightness on my brow
And although it's been a while
That I've not given thanks
For my life
I am thankful that I've not forgotten how.

ONE DAY TEN MINUTES A THOUSAND YEARS

Visitors day
One day a week
We are allowed to talk
to the world outside
Voices at once unfurl
through twenty or so holes
Our Black backs bent
if we want to speak
or be heard

One day a week in a steelpaneled room
I look through greasestained
Thickglass window
and try to wipe the smudge
Away from the face I see
The face that looks back and sees
the smudge on me

For ten minutes
One day a week
We line up seven in a row
And yell through perforations
in steel
While we bend, strain to hear
To get a look at those
Who come to see us
Yell at them.

SOMETIMES THE POEMS
DON'T WANT TO COME

Sometimes the poems seem like
They don't want to come

Thoughts won't be born
Because there is no love in them

Creativity
Just a few dead seeds
On a stone in the sweltering sun

4. Stop Time

A POEM FOR BLACK RHYTHMETICIANS

The drum is the heartbeat
Of Mother Africa
As she shapes life and
Gives birth
To the world

Sun sings the tempo up and down
From the days of old
In the kingdoms of Ghana, Songhai and Mali
When the drum called
The Council of Elders and the community
Together

The drumbeat counted the stars
As hearts rested after a weary day
Of hard work and heavy worry
The drum made the rhythm of Black love
That is why
Our hips know so well
How to make Black babies, honey suckled

The drums sounded the warning
    Oppressors are coming
    Oppressors are coming
And when slavers discovered
How much we communicated
With music they could not understand

They took up our drums
But not our rhythm

Our songs grew in dungeons and cottonfields
And when we had no drums
We got some hambones
And beat on hollow tree trunks in the woods
And we danced
When the devilman buried our bones
We slapped our thighs and told the message
　　Hambone hambone have you heard

Now Olatungi and Max Roach
Big Black and Elvin Jones
All know the rhythm
That we brought with us from Africa
They know how to unleash the sound
Of a celldoor slamming shut
They know the tremble, the cymbal sound
When needles of dope
Are mainlined to our brains
Our drummers know the sounds
Of glass breaking in our teeth
And sometimes in our eyes
They know silence
They know the emptiness where once
We had visions of light

Our drummers know the sounds
Of death beating at our brows
From Watts to North Carolina

They know the gnawing sound
Of a rat nibbling on a Blackchild's mouth
Drummers know we are flooded with trouble
They know Africa is still raging
in our blood

Black drummers know
History is in our heartbeats
Liberation is its tune
Tempo singing
Now for freedom is not too soon
Now for freedom is not too soon

FOR ALICE COLTRANE

Karma itself
Has given you
Love to give
And
Thru your fingertips
I have felt enlightenment

Your touch given to me
In a chalice of gold
Inlaid with rings of ebony

The life you offer
Is Karma's dew

What a woman you must be
Coltrane having loved you

MUSIC MAKERS IN THE DARK

Blind Tom
Al
Ray
Rahsaan
Stevie
Wonder what all of you
Could see in this poem

Could you, Blind Tom
Take the sound
Out of this cell
And change it into a
Symphony of freedom?

And you, Al Hibler,
Can you add to the symphony
Just like you did
When I heard you sing in Harlem
At the Apollo?

Ray,
You've sung Moon Over Miami
And I've hardly seen the moon

Sun or stars
Since I've been caged here

Could you, Ray
While tenderly caressing that ivory
The way you so spiritually do
Could you sing some blues
About the dues I'm paying?
Could you bring me out
Of this oppressive gloom
Breaking a tune
Down to its knees
And have it holler
Freedom?

And Rahsaan,
Could you remember when
I held your hand
And touched your shoulders?
Could you hear me saying
That if I could help it—
And I'll try—
To keep our spirits
Our music alive
To help with my poems
To make sure it survives?

Could you write me a tune, Rahsaan
Called the Double Cross
Because you know what the rugged cross
The burning cross

And getting across is all about?
Could you use your nose flute
And make it sing of flowers?
Could you somehow let me
Have your eyes
For just one hour?

Stevie,
I recall your sound
As red rosepetals
Gave way to the summer
Gave way to a woman's soft kiss
Gave way to a moment
That invited me to enjoy
The rise and fall
Of love's surprise
Stevie, could you sing a few notes for me,
So I can learn my way around this feeling?

Black music makers
With your sound and sight
Make some light
A way out of this dungeon
Today, tonight

ON READING NIKKI GIOVANNI

Soul stirring feeling in hand tonite
And in my eyes and shaking my shoulders
The confident restlessness in you
Expressed in words that soothe and arouse

The cold of March snow between
The warm pages
And here I am
Scars down my viscera
Here I am
Near the sight of old women pissing
On themselves and where a child
Died yesterday

Militancy your claim Nikki
With defiant words that bend
The devil's fork into a shovel
For him to dig his eventual end

Your fortitude makes it possible for you
To recover quickly from words
Your beauty is shielded with an aura
Of sensitiveness that intensifies
The passion I feel within your eyes, your smile

To you Nikki loving in a Black way
To your words that reflect your intensity

What that in your calabash
Black woman so fine
What that in your loving smile
Is it a melody of Black moments
Songs of our spiritual past
Brought back and rejoiced by you in poems

You feelings are fine
Fine as a Black velvet thread
Sewn into this society's decaying fabric
Your judgment the poems that made this one

POEM TO ROBERT KAUFMAN

Last night I heard of you, your poems
Last night I heard another way
To ward off the grit, the grind
Last night I heard how
You kept the foot of time from
Kicking your head in and future out
Your poems pronounced my scope
Scars, sores, drunken stupors
Narcotic afflictions, hazy aftermaths
Jails, blood baths and brutality multiplied

Your words written to blues and jazz
Just like at times I feel my fate
You wrote

"Think I'll put my eyes on a diet
My tears are gaining too much weight"

You wrote just like you knew
And you must have, too,
"What good are poems?"

How I long for the sun,
The atmosphere is so frigid here
Last night I wrapped my mind
Around the bars
Shook nothing but some anguish out of me
Maybe

But here I am still shaking inside
Like a drunk with delirium tremens
And your words record my dilemma
You wrote
"I am apprehensive about my future
"My past has turned its back on me"

Last night when the jailers came
And made us move so I could not
See or hear your poems
I knew what you meant when you wrote
"Madness is a summer resort for cave men"

Thought I saw thru the bars
Lady Day and Yardbird
Thought I heard it said
You had disappeared

That you were nowhere to be found
That you were suffering from
"A suicide of the soul"

What for the poet is there to look for
When life can't or won't reappear in poems?

I will read more of you, where
When and if I can
Write you a blues and jazz poem
Absorb myself in your reflections
Be free slave, free enough to create
Altho with subdued glee
I'll be free slave, free enough
Instead of writing it
Be
Poetry

THE X IN XMAS

She spends the winter flat broke
Her children shivering from the
Choking cold and asking what will
They get for Christmas

Cheap ornaments dangle seductively
From her ears and arms and waist

She dreads the sight of the ceiling
She dreads the crashing and crawling
The pawing the dirty sheets and
The filthy walls
And the slobbering that
Leaves sticky spills down her thighs

She buys a wilted tree
And hangs her tinseled earrings on it
She puts surprises
And laughter under it
But not without weeping

She knows the meaning of the X
In Xmas

QUEEN CITY

Along Trade Street late at night
Wears are exchanged
The sights come out in
Flimsy nightgowns and knit
Tight fitting pant(ies)

Brothers dressed like sisters
eyelashed highheeled long fingernailed
Necklaced powdered rouged
Bloused and braceleted down

With sweety this darling sugar that
With baby this and honey this gawk
On Trade Street they prance
With switchy movements effeminate walk

The beauty of Blackness
Made a mockery of
On the TV screen
A number one scene
Is Flip Wilson turning into Geraldine

Our beauty as Black warriors mischanneled
It finds men turning to perfumes
g strings and impersonations
Instead of liberation

They don't call Charlotte, North Carolina
The Queen City for nothing.

COUNTENANCE POEM
ON MAKING FOUR WAYS TO
SURVIVE OUT OF ONE*

Through the cracks and crevices of time
In on and around: these walls scream
The clanging noise that crawls continuously
Inside these depressing halls
The slamming doors upon my ears
Squeezing my body to break me
My eyes search out in this horror chamber
My cramped hand makes or takes notes
There is no place for smiles here
Moment after moment the future denies
I've heard screams
I've heard cries seething with anguish
I hear the thud and crash and bang
Always hearing somebody crumble
Thrown into blockade after blockade
Word of condemnation and abandonment constant
I slip back into time's crevices and cracks
In the abyss of time as I feel it now
Sandwiched between concrete sky and land
Wounds multiplied spiritually I survive

* With thanks to Amon Liner

Society falling apart at the seams
Justice pressures for a false confession
Forbidding slashing clawing mauling
Intending to silence and destroy Justice bolts
Pinching my nerves tightening
Like a vice grip
Millions of lives forgotten here
I write eulogies in choking air
The pressure constricts my thoughts
In the corners I hear bones rattling
From time suffocating in rib cages
Movement stifled with inactivity
Depression hammering at me again
Confess crazy nigger to the lie or die
Sundown is a life sentence here
We hate you nigger and want to kill you
For shelter in the shadows
I reach out and hold a poem by the hand
Invisible chains less heavy and abusive
Justice locks me away ungrateful unfaithful slave

DESIRE IN HAND

Inmates, some of them,
walk around parading their penises
putting their joints into each other's faces
and when unable to shake off the remembrance
of pleasure from their bones,
they hold themselves in hand,
sliding their squeezed palms
over swelling desires,
their bodies under covers
make tents as they pull rhythm
in the wrinkle of semenstained sheets,
their trembling, muffled groans,
remnants of sighs, flushed away later as
orgasms in toilet paper

Next day one tries to switch sheets with another
In an effort to conceal his need

TIME SQUEEZE

The time here
Pressures thoughts
Like thumb

And index finger
Squeezing
A toothpaste tube

I AM MAN, NOT MANIKIN

I am man, not manikin
My claim to this based on
My human gender
My birth as manchild
X chromosome emerging
Instead of Y

I am man, not manikin
My mother Africa told me no differently
But here I am subdued, dehumanized
Victim of the penis myth
Because I love life and freedom so deeply

I am man, not manikin
Refusing to be programmed
By the insanity of a warped minded society
Where perversity is big business

I am man, not manikin
Wanting liberation from oppression
And the same death white woman

Would be subjected to if she were not
The propagator of oppressors' offspring

I am man, not manikin
I've known for centuries
That even white women
Have been known to drool
Watching me lynched
Smile while I'm dying
Waiting for a souvenir—
My tooth, my ear

I am man, not manikin
Been kin to dummy too damn long
Been acting stupid far too long
Forced into caricatured expression
Just like the cigar store Indian
Or the lifesize smiling mammy doll
In front of some rebel flag selling store

I am man, not manikin
Trying to hold onto my humanness
Wanting to continue emotions
Mingling, tingling, melting, soaring
With woman I respect
Not as book or baby maker
Not as someone always on her back

I am man, not manikin
Not willing to be deprived
Of time to love or live

Not willing to be drowned, confused
In some bottomless pit

I am man, not manikin
A Black man real and proud with it.

KWANZA*
A POEM TO BLACK YOUTH

You are the life and breath
Of breath itself
Young Black minds
With many memories to learn
Harambie
Gather
The knowledge about yourself with
Ujima
You with the time to
Take the time
Take the time
And make your life
Uhuru

---

* *Kwanza*—First
  Harambie—Meeting place
  Ujima—Collective work and responsibility
  Uhuru—Freedom

5. Space That Confines

ABOUT THE AUTHOR

T. J. REDDY, the first of nine children, was born in Savannah, Georgia, on August 6, 1945. Moving to New York at the age of fourteen, he graduated from Boys High School in Brooklyn in 1963. In September 1964, he entered Johnson C. Smith University in Charlotte, North Carolina. After transferring to the University of North Carolina at Charlotte in 1968, Reddy became poetry consultant, then associate editor of the campus arts magazine. He was winner of the University's first creative arts award. A play by Reddy, *The Meet*, was produced at the college and later in the community.

Reddy's poems have appeared in the *Red Clay Reader*, *Southern Poetry Review*, *A Galaxy of Black Writing*, *Human Voices*, *Eleven Charlotte Poets*, and other magazines and anthologies. He was coeditor of *Aim* magazine. In 1968 he married Vicky Minar. They live in Charlotte.

The pencil drawings in the book were done on scrap paper in the Mecklenburg County Jail. The jacket illustration, "Reflections: A Self-Portrait," done in acrylic on canvas, was inspired by the poem "Bloodsmiles" by Black poet Don L. Lee. In Reddy's own words, "The bars symbolize Black and White 'people' who are responsible for my imprisonment . . . The white in the painting overhead indicates the sterility of White America, how it de-emphasizes, whitewashes . . . oppression. The red at the base of White America symbolizes rage, cruelty, murder in the name of power and progress. The hands gripping the bars symbolize how I am now caged in a cell, but that society is as oppressive outside the physical confinement as it is inside it."